Contents

William Collins' dream of knowledge for all began with the publication of his first book in 1819.
A self-educated mill worker, he not only enriched millions of lives, but also founded a flourishing publishing house.
Today, staying true to this spirit, Collins books are packed with inspiration, innovation and practical expertise.
They place you at the centre of a world of possibility and give you exactly what you need to explore it.

Collins. Freedom to teach.

Published by Collins
An imprint of HarperCollins*Publishers*
The News Building, 1 London Bridge Street, London, SE1 9GF, UK

HarperCollins*Publishers*
Macken House, 39/40 Mayor Street Upper, Dublin 1, DO1 C9W8, Ireland

Browse the complete Collins catalogue at
www.collins.co.uk

© HarperCollins*Publishers* Limited 2021

10 9 8 7 6 5 4 3

ISBN 978-0-00-846889-7

British Library Cataloguing-in-Publication Data
A catalogue record for this publication is available from the British Library.

Compiled by: Fiona Macgregor
Publisher: Elaine Higgleton
Product manager: Letitia Luff
Commissioning editor: Rachel Houghton
Edited by: Hannah Hirst-Dunton
Editorial management: Oriel Square
Cover designer: Kevin Robbins
Cover illustrations: Jouve India Pvt. Ltd.
Additional text credit: p 3–11 Lucy Courtenay,
p 12–13, 22–23 Fiona Macgregor p 14–21 Maoliosa Kelly,
p 24–31 Clare Helen Welsh
Internal illustrations: p 3–11 David Hill, p 14–21 Beccy Blake,
p 24–31 Valeria Abatzoglu
Typesetter: Jouve India Pvt. Ltd.
Production controller: Lyndsey Rogers
Printed and Bound in the UK using 100% Renewable Electricity
at Martins the Printers

Acknowledgements

With thanks to all the kindergarten staff and their schools around the world who have helped with the development of this course, by sharing insights and commenting on and testing sample materials:

Calcutta International School: Sharmila Majumdar, Mrs Pratima Nayar, Preeti Roychoudhury, Tinku Yadav, Lakshmi Khanna, Mousumi Guha, Radhika Dhanuka, Archana Tiwari, Urmita Das; Gateway College (Sri Lanka): Kousala Benedict; Hawar International School: Kareen Barakat, Shahla Mohammed, Jennah Hussain; Manthan International School: Shalini Reddy; Monterey Pre-Primary: Adina Oram; Prometheus School: Aneesha Sahni, Deepa Nanda; Pragyanam School: Monika Sachdev; Rosary Sisters High School: Samar Sabat, Sireen Freij, Hiba Mousa; Solitaire Global School: Devi Nimmagadda; United Charter Schools (UCS): Tabassum Murtaza and staff; Vietnam Australia International School: Holly Simpson

The publishers wish to thank the following for permission to reproduce photographs.

(t = top, c = centre, b = bottom, r = right, l = left)

p 12 yampi/Shutterstock, p 13tl Pakmor/Shutterstock, p 13tr everydayplus/Shutterstock, p 13bl noprati somchit/Shutterstock, p 13tr JIANG HONGYAN/Shutterstock, p 13–4 Wira SHK/Shutterstock, p 14, 16, 18, 20 Antony Elworthy

Splash!

SPLASH!

What is it made of?

wall

window

table

blanket

wood

cloth

glass

bricks

What am I?

A doctor

What am I?

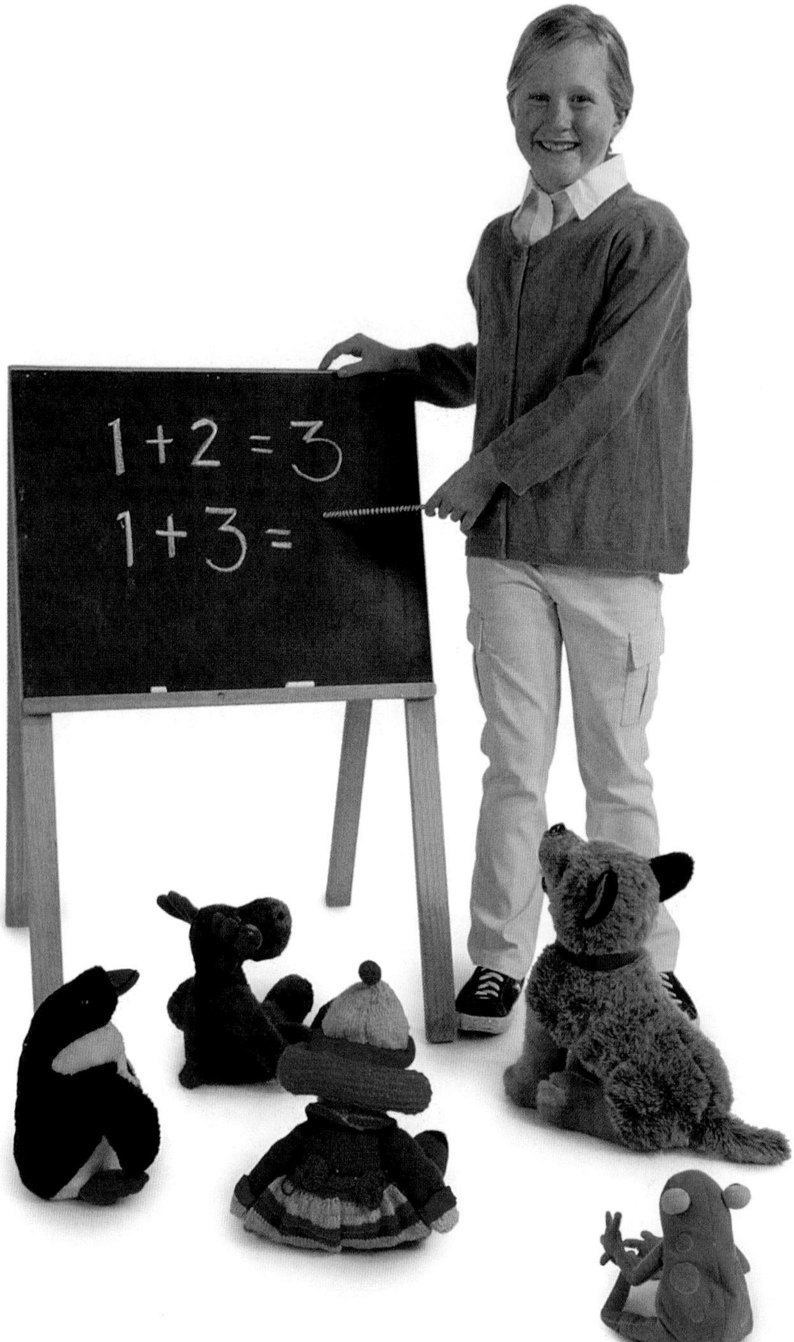

A teacher

What am I?

A postman

What am I?

A builder

In the park

up

down

under

with

in

on

Chat, chat, chat!

Dad can chat to Mum.

Jan and Gran can chat.

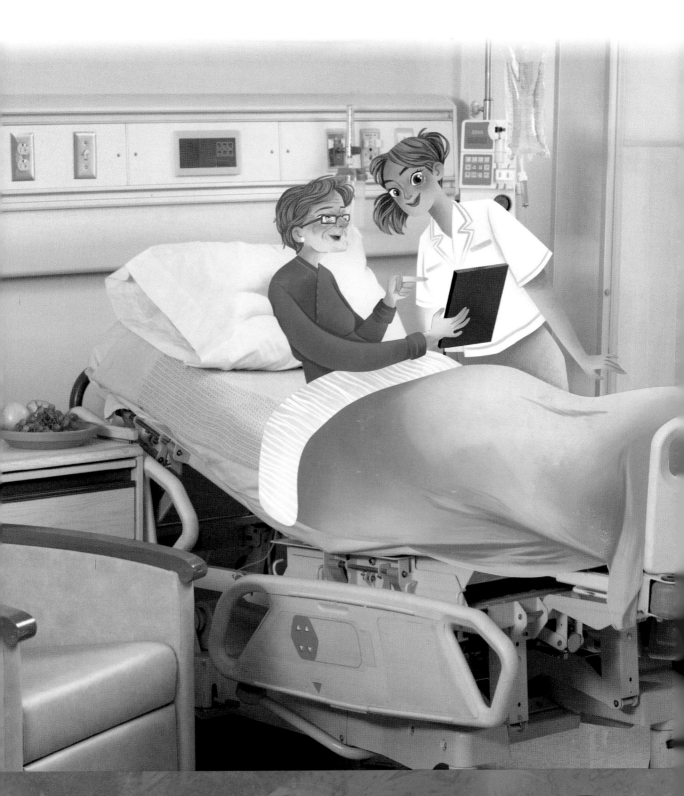

I can chat with Ming.

We can all chat!

Reading notes

Story	Sounds	Language structures
Splash!	'e' 'c' 's' 'n'	Saying what the weather is (cloudy, rainy, sunny, windy); using *I can see a...*
What is it made of?	'w' 't' 's' 'm'	Describing what things are made of: *It is made of...*
What am I?	't' 'p' 'b' 'd'	Identifying jobs: *I am a...*
In the park	revision	Saying where things are: *in, on, over, under, behind, in front of*
Chat, chat, chat!	'ch'	Talking about technology; *I can chat...* (on the phone, on a tablet, on a computer)

When you read these stories to your children at home, point out the new sound(s) in each story. Ask: *What sound is this? What letter is this?* Encourage your child to find the letter on the page. Then get them to say the sound, and the word, out loud.

Practise these language structures by asking questions. For example, ask: *What is it made of?* to elicit the response: *It is made of (material)*; or ask: *Who am I?* and point at the photograph on page 18 to get the answer: *I am a postman.*